Rooted in Resilience

"Surviving the Pressure on the Pathway to Purpose"

By:
Dr. Christina Monford-McNish

All rights reserved.

This book, or parts thereof, may not be reproduced, distributed, transmitted in any form, by any means, without permission in writing from the author.

Copyright ©2023 Dr. Christina Monford McNish

Published by
Live Limitless Media Group

Publishing@sierrarainge.com

info@livelimitlessmedia.com

Dr. Christina Monford- McNish
Contact Information

Email: rootedinresiliencellc@gmail.com

Website: www.rootedinresiliencebook.com

Printed in the United States of America

ISBN: 978-1-952903-47-2

Library of Congress Number: 2023920738

Dedication

This book is dedicated to my late mother who birthed me, my husband who believes in me and supports everything I do, my children who have made me the mother I never had and to the many people that can relate to the many obstacles that I share in this book.

v

Acknowledgements

I would like to acknowledge so many people from my childhood who took me in as if I were their own. First, my sister "Tezlyn Wallace", who practically raised me for the first four years of my life. She even took me on dates with her. To my godmother, "Gwendolyn Ervin Nmezi" who not only took me in, but also gave me exposure to the great field of dentistry. My god sister "Danyuell Newkirk " who stepped in as a big sister taught me how to lay my first track of hair extensions that compelled me to grow my love for styling hair; and who also inspired my enthusiasm for festive Christmas celebrations. To my brother's mother, "Sandra Massey-Gates", who also took me in a few times and always made me feel like I was a part of her family. To my neighbors, "LaVonne and Rosemary James' 'who opened their hearts and their home to me multiple

Acknowledgements

times, kept me fed and would even send me back home with bags of groceries; I am eternally grateful for your love and generosity. To my father's sister, my Auntie-grandma "Annie (Shortie) Watson" and cousin "Shirley Oliver" who always granted me an open door, and my neighbor "Lakesha Canady", "Linda Allen" (Rev. Edward and Mary Norman) (Deneane Campbell, Joya Allen, Andrea Campbell-Dingle), this family not only took me in a few times, but also initiated my walk with Christ and my baptism. I'd also like to acknowledge another next-door neighbor "Shauna Washington" (Shanqeita and Deuntaye Sellers) who also provided me with love and shelter during my time of need. To my elementary school best friend Julia Kittles-Holloway's grandmother "Helen Bright" who offered me love and a place to stay for over a year, to my Auntie Cousin "Josie Smith" who was there since birth and is the reason I love caress soap today; her daughters, my cousins "Rena and Tracey Smith" who also stepped in from time to time when I was in need of support in these transitions. I'd like to thank another neighbor who lived across the street who took me in when our electricity was out "Sharon (Miss Kitty) Williams", (Crissy Simmons-Green and Daryl Thomas) this is where I learned how to cook grits. I moved in with my middle/high school best friend "Dishan Brant" and her mother "Patricia Copeland-Gaulden". To our high school PTSA mom "Mrs. Cheryl Owens" Thank you for taking me out of class to ensure that I applied to college. I entered a local program called DANIEL where my counselor Mr. McNeil played a pivotal role as I navigated as an independent adolescent.

There have been so many amazing people throughout my journey who have granted me love, compassion and support. I am who I am today because of your willingness to step in and offer your kindness, your homes and your hearts. I am extremely grateful for every kind word, warm hug, open door and loving guidance. When I reflect on my blessings, I begin with each of you.

Thank You!

Acknowledgements

> *"Destiny is not a matter of chance;*
> *it is a matter of choice.*
> *It is not a thing to be waited for,*
> *it is a thing to be achieved."*

Table of Contents

Dedication iii

Acknowledgements v

Introduction 1

Chapter One: "Destiny Decisions" 17

Chapter Two: "Crowned with Purpose" 25

Chapter Three: "Fix Your Crown: Heal the Root" 37

Chapter Four: "Polished and Perfected" 47

Chapter Five: "The Divine Nine" 55

Chapter Six: "Rooted in Relationships" 63

Chapter Seven: "Faith, Focus & Family" 73

Chapter Eight: "Driving Destiny" 79

Rooted in Resilience Daily Affirmations 85

Rooted in Resilience Mindset Guide 93

About the Author 99

Acknowledgements

Introduction

Chaos is often the place where creativity is crippled, potential is sabotaged and destiny is derailed. It's a place void of order where calamity thrives and struggle is at the forefront of daily survival. While chaos is known for disorder and the detriment that it breeds; there are some instances where chaos creates unrelenting resilience, unwavering tenacity and an instinct to survive that becomes a catalyst to thrive. When I reflect on my life, I am overwhelmed with gratitude. Today I am a successful dentist leading a team of dental experts, making a huge impact in my local community and running a 7-figure practice that has allowed me to disrupt poverty, break the cycle of trauma, build a beautiful and healthy family while pursuing a life of purpose. Statistically, this is not supposed to be my life. By most measures, my success

Rooted in Resilience

story is a mere miracle; not because I didn't possess the skills, intellect and talent to succeed, but because of the destructive path I've had to navigate to get here.

I was born to two parents, both of whom were highly skilled and intelligent professionals. However, my mother faced significant challenges due to her battle with drug and alcohol abuse, and my father's brilliance was overshadowed by his involvement in drug distribution.

He was a licensed pharmacist and Alumni from Florida A & M University which housed one of the most reputable pharmaceutical programs in the nation. After graduating, he was drafted into the U.S. Army where he served as captain for over eight years and fought in the Vietnam War; after being honorably discharged from the Army, he later opened up his own drugstore which unfortunately became his hub to distribute illegal drugs. He started selling cocaine which destroyed many predominantly black inner-city communities in the seventies and eighties during former President Reagan's

Introduction

war on drugs. My father ended up losing his license and was a large-scale cocaine distributor when he met my mother who at the time was addicted to the substance.

I was birthed through the bond of my mother's addiction and my father's illegal cocaine distribution career. I entered the world shaking from the effects of substance withdrawals as I exited my mother's womb. This was a popular phenomenon in the black community during that time and was often referred to as "crack babies." Thankfully, I didn't suffer any brain development or other biological or physiological delays. After surviving the infancy withdrawals, I went on to have a normal developmental process despite medical statistics that would predict otherwise. My mother's addiction rendered her unfit, so growing up, my sister who is 14 years older than me was my primary caretaker. When my sister became of age, she moved out and never looked back. When she left, my life went into a downward spiral and I bounced around from house to house, moving in with anyone who was willing to take me in. My older sister was my only source of stability and while I know she left as a desperate means to ensure her own survival, her vacancy was felt everyday as the abuse, neglect and trauma increased in her absence.

My mother's addiction went from bad to worse and she no longer made any attempts to hide her drug use. She would smoke her crack pipe, get extremely intoxicated and pass out on the floor right in front of me. I learned how to work around her inadequacies; as a kindergartener, I would get myself dressed and go off to school on my own. School became not only my escape, but my safe haven. My teachers were the only positive influences in my life and I looked up to them as my role models. As a successful professional today, I'm often asked who inspired my career choice, or what were my sources of inspiration along the way; It's often a full circle moment when I'm led to answer these sorts of questions because although my parents were navigating the struggle and

Introduction

strain of the street life; they inspired my career. While my father was a licensed pharmacist, my mother was a dental technician who made illegal dentures out of her home. My parents didn't make the best choices and they didn't properly nurture their gifts and talents; drugs have a way of deterring and downright destroying dreams; but despite their limitations; they still exposed me to the possibility of earning a professional career. Watching them, I knew I wanted to pursue a career that would be respected but I desired for it to also be integral. I didn't want to have to look over my shoulder or operate underground. I excelled academically and some of my most fond memories with my parents, although minimal, are moments where they made efforts to impart wisdom into me. I can remember spending time with my father and he would drill me on my knowledge of math. He would say, "how many inches are in a foot? How many feet are in a mile? And he would expect a swift and accurate answer from me. I looked forward to these moments with my father and they instilled in me a love for learning and math.

Perhaps, I cherished these times with my father as they were very few and far between. For the most part, he was absent in my life, mostly showing up to check in and give money to whoever had taken me in at the time. Most of the people who opened their doors to me were those who lived in my neighborhood and were aware of my mother's addiction, my father's absence as well as my living conditions. Some of them felt sorry for me and wanted to help, others saw it as an opportunity to get drugs or money from my father as payment, while the most vile used it as an opportunity to exploit my vulnerabilities and further abuse me. I would usually spend the weekend at someone's house and that weekend turned into 8 months or a year; I would stay there until my mother came for me. Throughout my childhood I moved into over 20 different neighborhoods on the northside of Jacksonville, FL.

As I started to mature and physically develop, I became a target for my mother's acquaintances who were also strung out on drugs or dealers of drugs. While she was

Introduction

getting high or passed out in the room next door, they would often make their way into my room to touch me or make me touch them. This was the norm and I had become accustomed to being violated. Growing up, I never really felt safe; and I lived my life in a constant state of flight or fight mode. I was either being abused, neglected, robbed, manipulated or sexually assaulted. I learned how to survive under these sorts of harsh conditions by going out of my way to make myself as small and as invisible as possible. Whenever I was taken in by someone, I would eat very little, clean baseboards, wash clothes, wipe down China, cook and anything else I could do to make sure I wasn't a burden. I developed a fear of rejection as a result of never really having a safe place to belong. I later developed a love for styling hair and that became my side hustle to make money. I began to do hair for the people I lived with, family members and then I developed a small clientele of returning clients.

Throughout the years, this cycle of unstable and uncertain living conditions would continue. After being exposed to drugs and sexual behavior early on, I began to explore sex on my own. Looking back, I realize that I was searching for love, acceptance and a place where I felt like I could belong. I looked anywhere that resembled what I believed at the time was an authentic expression of affection. This search for love that my inner wounded, neglected and abused child sought after often turned up void, leaving me feeling more alone, used up, unworthy and emptier than ever. It wasn't until I was 12 and pregnant, I realized that when you have never experienced the nurturing, protection, comfort and care of a healthy early childhood and developmental experience, your definition and standard for love is often below the bare minimum of what you really deserve, and your perception of love is warped by the fact that you really don't have anything to compare it to in order to establish whether it is actually good. For me, any inkling of acceptance was love because after all, it was better than the feelings of neglect

Introduction

and rejection. I needed to feel desired, even if in the end I realized that all they ever wanted was the opportunity to have me sexually. I grew disappointed in the men around me who met my insecurities with their appetite for taking advantage of my naivety. Men who recognized my vulnerabilities as an opportunity to use me for their own pleasure. I wish that getting pregnant at 12 and having to experience the trauma of abortion would have been the thing that was a wakeup call to the adults around me who were responsible for my upbringing, but it wasn't. Life went on as usual, and I was left to fend for myself and survive the best way that I could. Only a year later at the age of 13 I was pregnant again this time by someone much older than me that I did not desire but found myself repeating the same traumatic cycle of abortion, inadequacy and even shame. I believed that I did not deserve life as I had aborted the opportunity for two of my babies to experience it. The heaviness of this truth weighed on me so much that I tried to take my own life. My attempts failed and I realized that my life had more purpose than I could see at the time. I was again, looking for sanctuary within people who didn't have good intentions for me.

This is when I began to understand the detrimental effects of searching for love and acceptance outside of yourself. I grew to become a rebel against suicide recognizing it to be the deceitful voice that we often fight with during moments of extreme personal criticism, and an inability to forgive ourselves. This was a defining moment in my life that is the foundation of my ode to resilience. Facing death and overcoming an attempt at my own life made me a renegade; I started rebelling against thoughts and feelings of suicide, unworthiness, inadequacy, self-doubt and fear. I boldly dared to live despite the pain of my past mistakes. I learned to give myself the same grace, compassion and forgiveness that I had so effortlessly offered to those who hurt me.

I was a young girl hell bent on survival, but this was a hard lesson learned that would serve me well in life. I started recognizing the fact that despite everything that I

Introduction

had experienced very early on in life, there was something deep within me that was still fighting. Part of it was of course for acceptance, but as I grew older, I began to desire not only love, but opportunity, safety, and success. I realized that these were things that I didn't have to wait for anyone to deem me worthy enough to provide for me and that I could manifest these things on my own. I was always a high achieving student who performed very well academically in school and after graduating high school I went on to attend Florida A & M University on a full academic scholarship.

Going away to college was a major life shift that felt like a fresh wind and new start to my life. It was the first time ever in my life that I felt a sense of safety and stability. I was able to begin the process of regulating my nervous system and focus without the constant strain of mere survival; I had gone through so much it was finally time that I could explore a new chapter in my life. I was surrounded by other young, bright and ambitious students who were also on a path of purpose, success and accomplishment. Not only was I able to gain a healthy and dependable support system through the University faculty and staff; but I gained an esteemed sisterhood through the incomparable Beta Alpha Chapter of Delta Sigma Theta Sorority Incorporated. Now, don't get me wrong, life as an undergraduate comes with its share of challenges, however, these challenges seemed like minor inconveniences compared to what I had already endured and conquered. I felt equipped to conquer and I did just that. During this time, I came to know a different version of myself and I finally discovered true love; self-love was the best love that I had ever known outside of the grace and mercy of God that had covered me and preserved me. Attending and excelling in college was a true turning point in my life. I recognized my identity beyond the trauma I had experienced; I gained a sense of personal value, belonging, acceptance and I began to explore my purpose. I started to extract lessons from my life vowing to use everything I had gone through as a tool for my own good.

Introduction

Every tear, ounce of shame and feelings of inadequacy or unworthiness would now be used as a catalyst for my own personal development. I gained a sense of empowerment, because although I had gone through the worst, I was able to look ahead with a vision for a life that was better. My past was not a means to define me, but conditioning to develop me.

Today I am living the life that my younger self dreamed of, prayed for and never gave up hope for. I am a broken, abused and neglected little girl's wildest dream. I no longer operate in survival; I have since transitioned into an operating system that allows me to thrive. Merely surviving is no longer the standard for my life. I am a proud stock owner of the largest dental service organization in the nation and lead & operate a very successful dental practice where I am able to serve my patients with excellence and contribute to my community with care and commitment. I have an amazing husband who continues to cocreate a healthy, loving, fun and romantic marriage where our priority is meeting one another's needs and building a beautiful life together. I get to raise healthy children who won't have to recover from childhood emotional injury. I have a strong network of sisters, friends, colleagues, staff and family who create an atmosphere where I feel seen, heard and valued. My environment and my relationships hold space for me to be my full self and they help me to thrive in authenticity.

Growing up, I constantly felt shame as I struggled to simply exist. Throughout the years, I have committed to healing through therapy, self-reflection, personal accountability and prayer. When the world counted me out and labeled me the daughter of a drug dealer and drug addict, a promiscuous teen, a child without a home; I chose to believe that I could be something much more and today my life is a reflection of that. Possessing the intrinsic ability to keep going, push forward, get up, try again, dust myself off, take another step, rise up, crawl if I had to, cry when I needed to and STILL press forward has been my superpower. In the moment I didn't recognize my power, I was simply fighting to survive. Today, I recognize that being *Rooted In Resilience* has been the firm foundation of my success today. I wrote this book, not only to share my story, but to be a living example of what is possible when you refuse to quit on yourself in the face of adversity. I wrote this book for every young girl around the world who refuses to be a victim because she knows that she holds the keys to victory within. To every young person who has been counted out because they don't look like, or come from an environment that mirrors success. For the underdogs who are fighting to create a life for themselves although their current circumstances don't reflect the life of their dreams. I know what it feels like to fight alone for a vision that no one sees but you. I know firsthand what it feels like to pursue success or change with the weight of shame, hurt, disappointment and the residue of abuse on your shoulders. I also know what it feels like to release your pain and alchemize it into purpose for your greater good. I wrote this book with you in mind. It doesn't matter where you come from or what you've been through; you have the power to reach deep within yourself and heal, transform, evolve, grow and change. This book is for the chain breakers, the underdogs, the victors who refused to be victims, the fighters and the survivors who are no longer satisfied with only surviving because they know their worth and have decided to thrive instead.

As you turn the pages in this book, I will share glimmers of my story that have had a profound impact on the woman I am today, along with the personal success principles, insights, lessons learned and values you can also implement into your life to create authentic success on your own terms. I am able to honor and celebrate the version of me that has been Rooted in Resilience, it was my sheer determination and commitment to growth that has allowed me to be crowned with purpose today. Allow this book to be your inspirational guide to live a life of purpose and impact.

Chapter One
"Destiny Decisions"

NAVIGATING THE PATH
LESS TRAVELED

*"Destiny is not a matter of chance;
it's a matter of choice"*

Destiny often appears as a distant and mysterious force that we look to with hope yet uncertainty. We believe that our destiny is a nostalgic predetermined end to the marathon that is our life's journey; but what we frequently underestimate is the profound impact of our decisions in shaping our realities and driving us toward our life's outcome. It's within the choices we make, the paths we choose to take, and the resilience we display against opposition that directly impact and reflect the life we have created through our decisions, actions and even at times our lack thereof.

Whenever I look back over my life, I realize that it was my decisions that have been the driving force of what my life is today, an unwavering presence that has pushed me forward, even when it was my own decisions that were holding me back at times. All of my choices; good, bad, wise, naive and even flat out wrong all have played a pivotal role in getting me where I am today. It is in those moments of opposition and adversity that we genuinely recognize the strength of our own character.

Discovering opportunity amidst opposition is a skill that can transform our lives. It's simple to become consumed by the pain of our past, to dwell on the mistakes and misfortunes that have brought us to our current situation. However, if we can find the wisdom to see beyond the pain, we may uncover the promise concealed within that silver lining. I've often found inspiration in the individuals who have guided me on my journey, the unsung heroes who recognized my potential when I couldn't see it in myself. Professors, teachers, coaches, neighbors, bus drivers - they all played a role in shaping my destiny. It's as though I was preserved with a purpose, guided by their support and belief in me. The journey towards destiny is seldom smooth. In fact, it can be a rugged path filled with obstacles, distractions, and setbacks. There were moments when it felt like the world was trying to pull me down, attempting to take advantage of my vulnerabilities. But it was during those times that I realized I possessed the power to steer my own destiny.

I shifted from being a victim of circumstances to becoming the author of my success story.

When you reclaim the power you hold over your own life, you in turn take accountability for the role you have played in your own suffering even if it was as a result of trauma, neglect or abuse inflicted upon you beyond your control. When you take inventory of your inner wounds, you know that although these unseen scars may reflect what you have gone through, they don't get to determine who you are and who you choose to be moving forward. It's about assessing your brokenness and choosing to heal. It's about recognizing your triggers and then choosing to respond differently; it's about learning to save and love yourself and no longer seek validation outwardly. It boils down to being bold and daring enough to have a vision for your life that scares you but liberates you at the same time.

The truth is, our lives are often a reflection of the choices we make and the action we take. At any point in your life you can begin to make better choices. Commit to making daily decisions that align with the life that you want to live.

In the grand scheme of life, it is the daily choices we make that ultimately shape the life we want to live. Our decisions, habits, and beliefs are the building blocks of our destiny, and they hold the power to transform our dreams into reality. Every single day, we are presented with a multitude of choices, some seemingly insignificant, while others carry profound consequences. It's in these choices that we find the true essence of our power, the ability to steer our lives in the direction we desire.

Imagine your life as a mosaic, with each small decision and habit contributing a unique piece to the larger picture. The belief that our choices don't matter until we make a big decision is a limiting belief that keeps you stuck. Every choice you make, from the moment you wake up to the moment you go to sleep, plays a role in shaping your destiny. For instance, the choice to start your day with a positive mindset and gratitude can set the tone for a day filled with opportunities and positivity. Conversely, succumbing to negativity and self-doubt can attract more of the same into your life.

Our daily habits are the foundation upon which our destiny is built. They are the actions we take without conscious thought, deeply ingrained behaviors that determine the course of our lives. Consider the power of habits such as regular exercise, healthy eating, and continuous learning. These habits not only improve our well-being but also contribute to our growth and success.

Rooted in Resilience

On the other hand, negative habits like procrastination, self-sabotage, and self-criticism can hold us back from reaching our full potential. Recognizing and altering these habits is a crucial step toward shaping a destiny that aligns with your aspirations.

Our beliefs are the lenses through which we view the world. They shape our perception of reality and influence the decisions we make. If you believe that you are capable of achieving your dreams, you are more likely to take the necessary actions to make them a reality. Ultimately, if you hold limiting beliefs that undermine your self-worth, you may inadvertently hinder your progress. To empower yourself in making destiny-driven decisions, it's essential to reinforce positive beliefs and cultivate healthy habits. Affirmations are a powerful tool for this purpose. Here are some affirmations to affirm your ability to make destiny driven decisions:

1. I am the architect of my destiny, and my choices matter.

2. I trust my intuition to guide me toward the life I desire.
3. Each choice I make aligns me with my dreams and aspirations.
4. I cultivate habits that empower and uplift me.
5. I believe in my limitless potential to create the life I want.
6. I release fear and doubt, replacing them with confidence and determination.
7. My daily choices lead me toward a future filled with success and happiness.

Repeat these affirmations daily to reinforce your commitment to making choices that align with the life you want to live. Remember that your destiny is not a distant, unattainable dream but a journey that unfolds with each decision, habit, and belief you embrace along the way. Embrace the power within you to shape your destiny, one choice at a time.

Rooted in Resilience

Chapter Two

"Crowned with Purpose"

EXPLORING INTENTIONAL IMPACT THROUGH LEGACY, LEADERSHIP AND COMMUNITY CONTRIBUTION.

"The purpose of surviving hard things is not just about getting through it; it's about blazing a path so that those coming behind you can see the way."

I celebrate every single person who has had to navigate hard moments and difficult circumstances in order to survive the things that have been designed to break them. Many first generation college students, first-in-the-family millionaires, first to move away, first to break toxic family cycles and even those first to choose a new path for themselves all have one thing in common; somewhere along the way, they discovered a sense of purpose that compelled them to push past limitations, heal childhood wounds, disrupt detrimental patterns, lean into faith, stand firmly on the belief of their potential in order to take inspired action towards the version of their lives that looked very different from where they'd come from. Not only does this take resilience, but it requires belief in oneself that it can be done.

During my time at Florida A & M University as an undergraduate student, I discovered that the traumatic experiences of my childhood had prepared me to withstand the pressures that accommodated the transitional experience into independent living that challenges most young adults during their passage from high school into college. While others were overwhelmed with the demands of managing their grades, social life, housing expenses, part time jobs and university clubs, I had become a master of multitasking and pushing through in the face of pressure. It was what I did well and it was also one of the greatest contributors to my success. While in college, I gained a sense of peace while most other students were trying to work through chaos. Chaos is where I thrived so I excelled in school and I was able to build many great relationships that are still serving me today. Without the mentorship and guidance of professors, my Sorors and other individuals who saw my potential and pushed me to live in it, I may not be the woman I am today. When I look back, I am grateful that I was able to benefit from grants, initiatives, and systems that were designed to help young men and women of color to excel in higher education. Scholarship, mentorship, and sisterhood held me up and pushed me forward on my journey towards obtaining my undergraduate degree. Understanding the impact that these have had in my life, I always said that when I got the opportunity to give back that I would. There are so many other young men and women like me who have had to survive abuse, neglect, exposure to drugs and violence and are yet gifted and capable of living a life that doesn't reflect all the hard things they've had to live through.

Rooted in Resilience

During my darkest times, hope was the light; when I wanted more for my life, the university atmosphere filled with young, bright and ambitious students was a daily reminder that greater was possible and I had what it takes.

My heart is with the young girl reading this book who dreams of a better future for herself, the young lady desperate for love and acceptance but searching for love in all the wrong places, the young man who didn't have a choice but to learn to hustle to survive in the streets but is intelligent enough to apply that same hustle towards a legitimate career if only he had an opportunity or guidance. To the many men and women who have had to heal from things that they didn't cause, forgive those who never apologized and fight for a chance to be somebody that their future self would be proud of. To those who are a byproduct of resilience and because of what they've learned along the way are uniquely skilled at managing massive success and overcoming major life obstacles. For those of us who have made it when the odds were stacked

- **Advocacy and Awareness:** Use your voice and platform to advocate for causes that matter to you, raise awareness and promote change.

- **Establishing Foundations or Programs:** Start initiatives that address specific community needs or support individuals striving to overcome similar adversities.

Steps Toward Meaningful Community Impact and a Purposeful Life

- **Identify Your Passion and Strengths:** Determine what causes ignite your passion and align with your strengths and experiences.

- **Find Collaborators and Allies:** Join forces with like-minded individuals or organizations to amplify your impact.

- **Take Action:** Start small and take consistent steps toward your goals. Every action, no matter how small, contributes to the bigger picture.

- **Measure and Adapt:** Assess the impact of your efforts regularly and adapt your strategies as needed to maximize effectiveness.

- **Cultivate Gratitude:** Recognize and appreciate the opportunity to contribute positively to your community. Gratitude fuels the drive for continuous impact.

Making a community impact and living a purposeful life is not just about the destination; it's about the journey. Embrace the opportunity to leverage your experiences, triumphs, and leadership skills to create a meaningful legacy that uplifts not only yourself but also those around you. Commit to being a beacon of change and a catalyst for a brighter, more empowered community.

Now let's talk about the importance of leadership. Today I lead a motivated team of twelve and a host of other dental professionals who rely on my guidance to run a thriving dental practice that is well established and celebrated for its community advocacy. Navigating struggle as a young girl prepared me to manage problems by confronting challenges with solutions. Adversity has an uncanny ability to sculpt leaders of unparalleled strength and resilience. Within the difficulty of challenge and pressure, individuals are pushed beyond their limits, forced to confront obstacles, and find solutions amidst chaos. It's within these trials that some of the most impactful leaders are forged, equipped with invaluable problem-solving skills honed under the weight of adversity.

Adversity acts as a catalyst for developing problem-solving skills under the most intense circumstances. When faced with challenges, those pursuing greatness often discover hidden reservoirs of creativity and resilience within themselves. The pressure cooker of adversity demands innovative and unconventional solutions, compelling individuals to think outside the box and navigate uncharted territories.

Beyond problem-solving, those who have weathered storms on their path to success possess a treasure trove of skills cultivated through adversity. These tools, when harnessed effectively, can elevate them as exceptional leaders:

1. **Resilience:** Adversity cultivates resilience, the ability to bounce back from setbacks and continue forward. Leaders who have overcome hardships are equipped with the resilience to face new challenges head-on.

2. **Adaptability:** The ever-changing landscape of adversity demands adaptability. Leaders who have navigated through tough times possess the agility to pivot strategies and approaches swiftly.

3. **Empathy and Compassion:** Struggles breed empathy. Leaders who have experienced hardship often possess a deep understanding and compassion for the challenges others face, making them more relatable and effective in their leadership.

4. **Decision-Making Under Pressure:** Adversity trains individuals to make critical decisions amidst chaos and uncertainty. Leaders who have weathered storms can make sound judgments even when the stakes are high.

5. **Vision and Determination:** Overcoming adversity fosters a clear vision for the future and a determination to achieve goals, which are essential qualities in effective leadership.

Tools to Leverage Struggle as Leadership Skills

1. **Reflection:** Take time to reflect on the lessons learned from past struggles. Analyze the skills acquired and how they can be applied to leadership roles.

2. **Seek Mentorship:** Learn from mentors who have navigated similar challenges. Their guidance can provide insights on leveraging adversity for leadership growth.

3. **Continuous Learning:** Embrace a mindset of continuous learning. Seek knowledge and skills that complement and enhance those cultivated through adversity.

4. **Storytelling:** Share your experiences and the lessons learned. Storytelling humanizes leaders and inspires others to overcome their own challenges.

5. **Mindfulness and Self-Care:** Ensure personal well-being. Leaders who have overcome adversity must prioritize self-care to maintain their strength and resilience.

Adversity, although daunting, can be a powerful catalyst for developing remarkable leaders. By harnessing the problem-solving skills and other invaluable tools cultivated through struggle, individuals pursuing greatness can leverage their past to lead effectively, inspire others, and create meaningful change in both their personal and professional spheres. This is the essence of resilience and a personal tribute to be crowned with purpose.

"Crowned with Purpose"

Chapter Three
"Fix Your Crown: Heal the Root"

PRIORITIZING HEALING AS
A SUCCESS STRATEGY

"Until you heal the wounds of your past,
you will continue to bleed"
~Iyanla Vanzant

As a highly successful dentist, my practice is known for its sought after dental cosmetic procedures. Patients often come to my office in order to enhance their smiles. While assisting them through various procedures to optimize the appearance of their teeth, my primary focus is on their overall oral health and hygiene. As a result of instant smiles recently popularized on social media that showcase overnight tooth perfection, more and more patients are prioritizing their tooth appearance and neglecting their oral health. Oral health is the leading pillar within my mission. Some patients who want to focus on the cosmetic procedures without first addressing the health and disease of their teeth and gums, have often sought out these treatments out of the country.

Healing the root cause of a tooth issue often involves addressing problems deep within the tooth, such as infection, decay, or damage to the pulp (the inner part of the tooth containing nerves and blood vessels) When a patient experiences tooth pain or discomfort, the first thing I do is examine the tooth and I must use a radiograph to identify the root cause. This step helps in understanding the extent of damage or infection within the tooth. If the root cause involves infection or damage to the pulp, I may recommend root canal therapy. During root canal therapy, the infected or damaged pulp is removed; this is where I use rotary instrumentation to clean & shape and irrigate the inner chamber and canal of the tooth. Afterwards, I fill and seal it to prevent further infection. This step is crucial for alleviating pain and preventing the spread of infection.

After a root canal, the tooth needs time to heal and I may prescribe antibiotics to clear any remaining infection and to ensure the area heals properly. This healing period allows the tooth to regain its strength and stability. Once the tooth has healed and stabilized, I then assess whether a crown is necessary to protect the weakened tooth. Sometimes, after a root canal, the tooth becomes more brittle and prone to fractures. In such cases, a crown becomes essential to strengthen and protect the tooth from further damage. Before placing the crown, any remaining decay or weakened structure on the tooth's surface is removed. This is where I ensure that the tooth is stable and healthy enough to support the crown, if and when I determine that it is, I proceed to prepare and place the crown securely over the treated tooth, providing added protection and restoring its functionality.

"Fix Your Crown: Heal the Root"

This comprehensive approach to healing or removing the root cause of a tooth issue involves resolving the underlying problem, such as decay or damage to the pulp, before proceeding with the placement of a crown. It ensures that the tooth's foundation is stable and healthy, allowing the crown to serve its purpose effectively.

You may not be interested in the crown placement protocol, but I promise there is a lesson in it. How many of us prioritize looking good in order to mask that we don't actually feel well? It's much easier to lace your face with foundation, concealer and blush to look the part, but what happens when you wash your face and all of the pain of your past, the trauma you've avoided, the fears you keep allowing to keep you stuck, the doubt that is delaying your destiny and the limiting beliefs that hold you captive to your negative self-talk are no longer hidden by your freshly beat face? Success is not just about looking the part, real success includes peace of mind, clarity of thought, and a healthy heart posture.

Rooted in Resilience

For many of us, offense and trauma was beyond our control, but even in instances where you were powerless during the commission of your pain, healing must be your responsibility. There are undoubtedly people who may be responsible for your pain, PTSD, depression or even anxiety, but healing is your portion. Today I am blessed to not only run a successful dental practice, but I'm a mom who is raising healthy, happy and well-rounded children. I get to experience the warmth, love and security of a healthy marriage while giving back to my community. On paper, my life looks amazing, but the truth is that it didn't always look or feel this way. There was a time when I was consumed with suicidal thoughts and I struggled to believe that my life was worth living. I'm so grateful for the tribe of people who surrounded me in love and lifted me with positivity so that I could survive those low moments. Mental and emotional wellness are pillars of true-life success. I was intentional about breaking toxic cycles and generational curses in my family and I knew that it would require prioritizing healing in my life. The fruits of my labor are evident today because I took time to face my trauma in order to experience triumph. I suffered for years from rejection, abandonment and neglect. These issues intensified in my intimate relationships. I was easily triggered by behaviors or conversations that remotely reminded me of the pain of being disregarded, left behind and not prioritized. This is when I became aware of attachment styles and how our early childhood development directly impacts how we engage in our adult relationships. I had to learn how to create a safe place within myself so that I could create a safe place for my family; so that I could have the capacity to be loving, whole and nurturing. I spent so much of my life in survival mode that I had to learn how to adjust to a mindset that allowed me to abandon the struggle, put my nervous system at ease and adopt a mindset that would allow me to thrive.

I know that there is a winner deep inside each of us. Too often, we are blinded by our purpose and potential because we are distracted by the pain that is blocking our view. Too many of us dress up our pain instead of truly dealing with it at the core. Much like a decaying tooth that must be treated before we are able to dress it up with a new crown, you must first heal the root cause of your personal inflictions in order to reach your full potential and operate at optimal functionality.

As you work towards healing the root of your pain so that you can establish your personal crown of purpose on a solid foundation; here are a few healing modalities that have helped me.

1. Seek out a professional: Therapy offers a safe space—a haven to unravel the complex thoughts, emotions and fears associated with past experiences. It's a tailored journey toward self-discovery, equipped with tools and professional insight designed to help you identify, explore and work through your issues.

2. Coaching, on the other hand, provides a roadmap for a specific goal like starting a business, building credit etc. coaching complements therapy by offering guidance, goal-setting, and accountability. Coaches help individuals identify barriers, set actionable steps, and cultivate a mindset conducive to healing, thus facilitating progress and personal growth.

3. Accountability: plays a pivotal role by fostering a sense of responsibility and commitment to one's healing journey. Being accountable to oneself or to a supportive group cultivates motivation, consistency, and progress, encouraging individuals to stay focused on their healing goals.

4. Self-reflection: promotes self-awareness by encouraging individuals to examine their thoughts, emotions, and behaviors. This practice allows for the identification of patterns, triggers, and

underlying causes of distress, aiding in the recognition and subsequent healing of past wounds.

5. Self-care: Self-care practices prioritize nurturing one's physical, emotional, and mental well-being. By engaging in activities that promote relaxation, stress reduction, and self-nourishment, individuals replenish their energy reserves, reduce anxiety, and enhance their overall resilience in the face of adversity.

6. Healing your Inner Child: Healing the inner child involves addressing unresolved emotions and traumas from childhood. This approach allows individuals to offer compassion and care to their younger selves, facilitating emotional healing and paving the way for improved self-esteem, healthier relationships, and emotional resilience.

7. Recognizing Triggers: Identifying triggers involves understanding and acknowledging stimuli that evoke distress or trauma-related responses. By

recognizing these triggers, individuals gain the ability to anticipate and manage their emotional reactions, leading to a sense of empowerment and control over their emotional well-being.

8. Commitment to Healing: Commitment to healing involves dedication and perseverance in the pursuit of personal growth and well-being. It entails embracing the healing journey as an ongoing process, fostering patience, self-compassion, and resilience amidst setbacks or challenges along the way.

Each of these modalities contributes uniquely to the healing process, offering tools, insights, and support that collectively foster emotional, psychological, and spiritual healing for individuals seeking to move beyond surviving to truly thriving in their lives. Remember, the path from survival to thriving is paved with courage, resilience, and unwavering commitment. When you decide that your future self deserves an opportunity to experience life without carrying the weight of your past, you in turn give yourself the gift of healing. This is when you alchemize pain into power and are able to coat what was once broken with a strong crown of purpose.

Chapter Four
"Polished and Perfected"

LIVING A LIFE
OF AUTHENTIC SUCCESS

"The most authentic version of success can be measured by how you've been able to transition from simply surviving to thriving"

There's an ongoing and unspoken but well recognized feud among those who are team Apple phone and their Android using counterparts. Now, essentially, both phones perform the same functions. They have comparable camera quality and competing features. While users from opposing sides of the device debate have compelling reasons why they believe their brand of choice is superior, the truth is that the phones may have similar qualities but it's the operating system that is different. Where you may swipe on your Apple device, in order to achieve the same result on an android may require a much different mechanism. They both take pictures, allow you to download and use most of the same apps and host wireless phone calls from anywhere in the world, however, it's the method in which you do each of these things that is the distinguishing factor. This is what I like to compare the difference between operating out of a survival mindset and a thriving mindset to. You can be in the same relationship, pursuing the same goals, have access to the same tools, be faced with the same conflicts; but the matter in which you deal with, engage in and manage each of these phenomenon's will be very different based on your state of mind. For example, when you are operating out of survival mode, your relationships are at risk for toxic behavior.

When you are stuck in survival mode due to past trauma or ongoing stress, it can significantly impact their relationships in various ways like communication challenges, trust issues, emotional distance, and difficulty with intimacy.

In survival mode, you may struggle to communicate effectively. You are more likely to be reactive, defensive, or withdrawn, making it difficult to express emotions or your needs clearly. This can lead to misunderstandings and conflicts in your close relationships. Living in a state of survival often involves a hyper-vigilant state, making it hard to trust others. Past trauma might create a constant sense of threat or fear, causing you to have difficulties trusting even those closest to you, leading to distance or strain in relationships. There is a high likelihood that you will struggle to connect emotionally, this may look like shutting down or detaching from feelings to protect yourself, which can create a sense of emotional distance or detachment in relationships. This also can inhibit your ability to be vulnerable and intimate, causing you to have barriers when attempting to form close connections, fearing vulnerability or potential hurt, which can hinder the depth and closeness in relationships.

When you shift into a state of survival, much like giving up your apple phone and converting to an Android device, you must now learn to exist and navigate the same functionalities using an opposing operating system. When you adopt a thriving mindset, it creates different outcomes in your life and relationships. This includes effective communication, the ability to build and give trust, the capacity to demonstrate emotional connection, and the ability to cultivate intimacy.

A thriving mindset fosters open, honest, and empathetic communication. When you exist and operate from a thriving state of mind, you are more likely to express yourself clearly, listen actively, and engage in constructive dialogue, leading to healthier relationships. You are better able to work on healing past wounds, which enables you to rebuild trust in yourself and those around you. This cultivates a sense of safety and security in relationships, fostering trust and deeper connections.

With a thriving mindset, you are more capable of connecting emotionally, embracing vulnerability; you are better equipped to navigate conflict in a healthy way leading to deeper, more fulfilling connections in relationships.

Overall, transitioning from survival mode to a thriving mindset allows you to address your past traumas, develop healthier coping mechanisms, and create a more secure emotional foundation.

This shift is not only necessary for you to experience an elevated way of existing, but it's the cornerstone of defining success on your own terms. When you are no longer a victim of your past, you can become the hero in your own life. When pain can no longer hold you back, you are free to create the life of your dreams.

Have you ever considered what your life would be like if you were no longer afraid of allowing others to get close to you? The funny thing about building emotional walls is that not only do you keep out the bad stuff, but you block goodness in your life as well. This is why it's better to establish boundaries than to build walls. Boundaries are not so much about keeping people and things away, but more so about keeping everyone and everything in their place. Your boundaries are a part of your personal success design. They help you determine what you want, what you refuse to tolerate, what inspires you, what fulfills you and what drains you.

It is up to you to decide which operating mode you will exist in. What I've found is that when I was operating from a place of survival, it allowed me to survive my struggle; but when I decided that I wanted to go higher and I began to heal, the same mechanisms, mindset, responses, behavior and language I used to navigate struggle were rendered useless and even downright counterproductive as I began to navigate a life free of trauma responses, toxic attachments, and poor mental and emotional health. There will come a time in your journey when you must give up the good in order to possess that which is great. Surviving my childhood was a good thing. I was able to develop resilience, conflict resolution skills as well as mental, emotional and spiritual fortitude, however, leaving behind my childhood survival instincts in order to adopt an elevated life protocol that allowed me to thrive instead of merely survive; now that's what I consider greatness. Simply put, what allows you to survive struggle must be adjusted in order to experience success and wellness on a higher level. You owe it to yourself to not only heal from the pain of your past, but to thrive, shine, evolve and grow!

Rooted in Resilience

Chapter Five

"The Divine Nine"

9 SUCCESS PRINCIPLES TO INCREASE RESILIENCE, MAXIMIZE IMPACT AND NURTURE GROWTH

"What you believe impacts how you show up in the world, the habits you form and the personal standard of excellence you establish in your life"

One of the greatest catalysts for growth are the relationships that sustain you and remind you of your power. They are the people who pour into you with genuine intentions mirroring your power and affirming your worth. When you have had to navigate and overcome trauma, you sometimes carry the residue of what you've lived through, overcome and survived. While resilience is the gift that fuels survival, relationships are the bridges that connect us to our potential. Being initiated in the Beta Alpha Chapter of Delta Sigma Theta Sorority, Incorporated, Fall 2003 as an undergraduate college student taught me the transformative power of sisterhood and how connection, support and community play such a major role in helping us to recognize and even live out our full potential. As I've continued to evolve, learn, unlearn, heal, and grow in my life, there have been some key principles that have stuck with me and served me at every level of my transformation. With an ode to the power of sisterhood, I lovingly refer to these personal mantras as the "divine nine" success principles to increase resilience, maximize impact and nurture growth. What we believe about ourselves, the world around us and even our potential directly impacts our behavior and how we show up in the world. These Divine Nine principles have guided me towards growth and I hope that they serve you as well.

1. **Manage Your Resources:** Overcoming tough times teaches us to use resources wisely. When you've faced scarcity, every little thing becomes valuable. You learn to be inventive, finding new ways to make the most of what you have. Managing resources means figuring out what's most important and focusing on that. It also teaches you to bounce back from tough situations and plan for the future. Sharing and working with others become essential too. Through it all, you learn to use things mindfully, avoiding waste and making the most of what's available.

2. **Take deliberate and determined action towards your goals:** Taking deliberate and determined action towards your goals is essential, especially after overcoming adversity. It's about moving forward with purpose and focus. When you've faced tough times, setting goals becomes a way to create a better future. Taking deliberate action

means making specific plans and following through on them. It's about being determined and persistent, even in the face of challenges or adversity.

3. **Face Opposition through the perspective of opportunity:** This principle is all about minimizing the mountains in your life through the power of perspective, and turning your lemons into lemonade. It's about recognizing every failure as an opportunity to learn and gain wisdom. Every loss that I endured was a lesson that helped me win later.

4. **Always Find the Will To Win:** What I've learned from my own experiences is that you will win if you refuse to quit. One of my favorite scriptures that reminds us of this truth is Galatians 6:9 which states, "let us not grow weary in well doing, for in due season we will reap a harvest if we faint not" This affirms that challenges may meet us on our

journey, but they don't have to beat us. Being determined and persistent towards growth amplifies our will to win, knowing that if we push through triumph is inevitable.

5. **Grace Factor:** Learning to extend grace has been a key pillar in my emotional and mental fortitude. Being unwilling to hold on to unforgiveness while offering compassion and empathy has helped me to not only release myself from the bondage of victimization and self-criticism. Not only do I practice being gentle with myself and giving myself as many second chances, as much grace and forgiveness necessary to move forward from setback and disappointment, but because I offer grace first to myself, I am able to extend it to others. Grace keeps us grounded and reminds us that even in our imperfection, we are still worthy and deserving.

6. **Making Healthy Connections:** Surround Yourself with People who have the capacity to celebrate you and not just tolerate you. For me this was sisterhood, community, and purpose partners along the way. Growing up, I found myself going from one family's couch to another. I moved around often and had to adapt quickly to different lifestyles as I moved from every household. Adaptability as a displaced adolescent, evolved into detachment as a young adult. In my intimate relationships, I learned how to detach and move on very quickly until I met someone that I didn't want to lose. These are the valuable relationships that mirror us and help us to recognize the areas that may require healing. Learning to make healthy connections positions you for long lasting, mutually beneficial relationships that sustain and inspire you, instead of draining you and reflecting the worst parts of yourself.

7. **Transcending from the survival mindset into an operating system that allows you to thrive:** Shifting from being driven by trauma to being governed by a mindset that compels you to navigate life outside the realm of perceived lack and scarcity is a must. Simply put, the survival skills that have aided you in reaching one level, will prevent you from reaching the next. In order to truly thrive, you must abandon the survival mindset and adopt a mindset that allows you to thrive.

8. **Overcoming the barriers of things designed to break you:** Heal from rejection, abandonment and neglect/ Show Up for Yourself. No 'one is going to treat you better than you. Learning to love yourself unconditionally, even the parts of you that seem unlovable. Rejection gave me fuel, I had something to prove to those who doubted me, to my circumstance, to society. When you've been

handed what looks like a losing hand, you must still find a way to win, even when winning appears unlikely. Rejection forced me to be my best self. In a sea of 100 "No's" I will overcome each wave until I land on the shore of a YES.

9. **Have an inspired vision for your future:** Who do you desire to become? What changes do you need to make to get there? Seeking out what you need in order to materialize the life that you visualize for yourself. You cannot be what you cannot see. See yourself winning, healed, happy, and succeeding. If you can visualize it, you can also materialize it.

Chapter Six
"Rooted in Relationships"

DEFINING THE CORE
OF WHAT CONNECTS YOU

"Human connection is the key to personal and career success"

When it comes to defining the core of our connections, we must first explore our own core values. What is it that you value? What is your personal hierarchy of values? How do these values impact your belief system and how does your belief system impact your behavior? What is defined at our core, creates a cycle and a blueprint for how we live our lives, the people we connect with, the bonds we build, the relationships we forge and the social, emotional and mental ecosystems that make up the world within us and around us. Our connections are established on common ground and that terrain is made up of our core values. When was the last time you took time to examine who you are at your core? What is your default response to conflict? Disappointment? Frustration? Fear? Success? Pleasure? Joy? Is your initial reaction to these stimuli a reaction of your traumatized self? Or your healed self? Now you may be asking yourself, what do my emotional reactions have to do with my relationships? Well, the answer is everything. Who you are at your core determines your capacity to connect with, engage, reciprocate and nurture healthy connections. Since we connect on common ground, and that common ground is often a reflection of our core values and beliefs, if we are still operating out of trauma and survival then we may find ourselves in a network built on trauma bonds and relationships that drain us. The relationships that matter the most to us may also suffer; we may find ourselves unable to be vulnerable, easily triggered or unable to work through conflict that arises in any relationship big or small. When we heal our core, our relationships are fortified. This is not limited to our personal relationships. It includes our relationship with money and our relationship with ourselves. As I evolved from a state of trauma, I became intentional about creating healthy dynamics in all of the relationships that were in my hierarchy of personal values. This included my relationship with my husband and my role as a wife, my relationship with my children and my role as a mother, my relationship with my siblings and my role as a sister, my relationship with community contribution and my role as a mentor.

Relationships sometimes require that we reevaluate our friendships and relationships to determine if they are actually working for us. When we find happiness within ourselves and we love and value who we are, our relationships will reflect that. It shows up in the way we clap for and celebrate others. We see it in the way we make sure we only maintain connections with people that have the capacity to celebrate us and not just tolerate us. We recognize it when we want to extend grace and forgiveness to others while also properly positioning them in our lives by limiting or prohibiting access to those who cause us harm. Much like we evaluate our goals yearly, we should also evaluate our relationships. Ask yourself, "Who showed up for me this year? Who can contribute to my growth by inspiring me to be my best self, and who takes away from that? Remember, you don't always have to cut people off, but you must properly position them in your life. I know in my life today, I need and value people who can clap for me, those I can be vulnerable with and are not secretly competing with me or wishing for my downfall.

When I decided who I wanted to be and how I wanted to show up in each of my roles within every relationship, I considered the healing modalities, mindset shifts, emotional availability, mental stamina and the needs of those I was in relationship with. I took inventory over those who were most important to me and what was necessary in order to nurture each relationship in a way that fulfilled me and served them.

When we talk about being rooted in relationships, we must mention that each relationship is like a seed and in order for it to grow in a healthy way, it must be rooted in good ground. We are the soil and our relationships are the seeds, when properly nurtured, our connections create a garden of resources, support, fulfillment, community and even purpose.

Take some time to explore and define your core values. When it's all said and done, what is it that matters the most to you? What issues are you passionate about? What community initiatives are you willing to champion? Is community contribution a part of your core values? What type of relationships do you desire to have in your life? Have you considered the types of connections that may benefit your life and propel you forward? Who do you need to be in order to connect with and nurture those types of relationships?

Rooted in Resilience

Examining core values and building relationships from a healthy core involves introspection, understanding personal values, and fostering connections based on authenticity and respect. Here are some tips to help you become rooted in your relationships by connecting to your core values.

1. **Self-Reflection:** Take time to reflect on your beliefs, principles, and what truly matters to you. Consider past experiences that have shaped your values and identify the core principles that guide your decisions and actions.

2. **Identify Core Values:** List and prioritize your core values. These could include honesty, compassion, resilience, or others that deeply resonate with you. Understanding your values helps in making decisions aligned with your authentic self.

3. **Authenticity in Relationships:** Build relationships based on authenticity and honesty. Share your

values and aspirations openly with others, encouraging mutual understanding and respect. Authenticity fosters genuine connections built on trust and understanding.

4. **Communication:** Effective communication is key. Express your values, needs, and boundaries clearly in relationships. Listen actively to understand others' perspectives and values, fostering a deeper connection based on mutual respect.

5. **Set Boundaries:** Healthy relationships thrive on mutual respect for boundaries. Understand your limits and communicate them respectfully. Encourage others to do the same, creating a space where both parties feel comfortable and respected. This helps to curate good soil for your relationships to grow.

6. **Empathy and Understanding:** Cultivate empathy by putting yourself in others' shoes. Understand that people may have different core values and

perspectives. Respect these differences while seeking common ground for healthy interactions.

7. **Consistency in Actions:** Align your actions with your values. Consistency builds trust and credibility in relationships. When your behavior reflects your core values, it strengthens the foundation of your connections.

8. **Evaluate Relationships:** Periodically assess your relationships to ensure they align with your core values. Healthy connections are those that support and align with your beliefs, contributing positively to your growth and well-being.

10. **Continual Growth:** Be open to growth and change. As you evolve, reassess your values and how they align with your relationships. Embrace personal growth while nurturing healthy connections that complement your evolving values.

By examining your core values and fostering relationships from a healthy core, you create a foundation that supports meaningful connections built on authenticity, good ground to perpetuate growth and personal fulfillment.

With your core values, goals, needs and beliefs in mind, take some time to take personal inventory of your relationships. Who are the most valuable people in your life, how does the connection between you benefit you, how can you nurture the relationship and reciprocate the value. Then consider what relationships may need to be repositioned. Maybe access needs to be limited or boundaries established. You are the CEO of your life; you get to choose your connections as you live an authentic life that aligns with your core values and helps you to remain fulfilled.

Rooted in Resilience

Chapter Seven
"Faith, Focus & Family"

BELIEVE THAT YOU CAN

*"She believed that she could,
so she did"*

Faith has grounded me and fueled me to achieve massive success. It has been my guiding light in a world full of uncertainty and it has kept me in the fight during the many moments when I felt like giving up. When I look back over my life, based on the environment I was raised in, the conditions I had to navigate, as well as the trauma, neglect and abuse I endured, I consider the fact that I am alive, well and in my right state of mind a mere miracle. Statistically, I could have turned out a number of ways, but grace, grit, grind, faith and focus have steered me towards a life of wellness, success and community contribution. I am so grateful to wake up and live the life that I worked so hard to build. In my life, I have always remained steadfast in my pursuit of my goals and I've been able to use both focus and faith as tools to reach every new level. When I was faced with the reality of my upbringing and the painful memories of many of those experiences, faith reminded me that my past had prepared me for my future and if I remained focused on where I was and where I was headed, I would eventually achieve my goals. Growing up, I didn't always know where I would get my next meal from, or how my future would play out. As a young and vulnerable little girl, I didn't know if I would get through the night without someone coming in at night and touching me inappropriately. For a long time, I felt like damaged goods, because I had been through so much at such a young age. I used to question if I would ever be a good enough woman. I wondered if there was anyone in the world who could love me wholeheartedly; it was faith that helped me to overcome this limiting belief and recognize that although I experienced some ugly things, I was yet and still beautiful, deserving and worthy of love, support, compassion, empathy and joy.

Even during stages of my life as a young girl working through trauma, it was the combination of faith and focus that were my weapons. I was a smart girl and school was my saving grace; it was my escape from abuse and my refuge from neglect. At school, I thrived, my teachers took notice and they even celebrated me. As I grew older and I experienced more stress, I noticed how whenever I was faced with a challenge, I would distract myself from the hard things by focusing on what came easy to me–school. I would often overcompensate in order to distract myself from things that brought me pain or discomfort. I learned to shift my focus towards things that I could control. At that time, I couldn't control the adults in my life or the decisions they made for themselves. I couldn't control my living arrangements or the cycle of abuse that I was able to witness around me; but I could control my time and what I chose to focus on. Focusing on academic success helped me to find something less painful to give my attention to and it served me well. Although I am no longer driven by trauma, focus is still my companion on my journey. It's no longer a trauma response or a coping mechanism, but a key to achieve success and execute my goals with clarity and efficiency. When I clearly identify what I want in my life, I can alleviate distractions that derail and deter me from my destination. I recognize distractions as anything, idea, goal, relationship, belief or behavior that gets in the way of my destiny. I believe that something bigger than myself has preserved me for a greater purpose and I'm committed to going the distance, making a massive impact and living a life of purpose and contribution. My faith tells me that I can do all things through Christ who strengthens me. My faith affirms that even when there is a mountain in front of me, there's a determined mountain climber within me. My faith says that I am healed, whole, powerful and positioned to live a life of success and progress. My faith reminds me that the same power that guided me through the valleys of neglect, abuse, and lack will lead me over every obstacle and through every test. I am focused on being the woman God had in mind when he created me and faith tells me that it's all possible.

Faith and focus has been my trusted companions and while this dynamic duo has been a faithful guide along my path, family has been the treasure that makes it all worth it. As I healed from trauma and released the grip that it had on me, it was important for me to create and nurture the family dynamic for myself that I never had but always dreamed of. Being able to reconnect with and build a relationship with my older sister who left home before me, and creating a healthy core family ecosystem with my husband and children is one of my greatest and most valued accomplishments and blessings. Through my marriage, I have learned first-hand the power of partnerships and how compatibility, mutual support, unconditional love, intimacy and grace sustains connections. My husband and I support one another's dreams and aspirations. We are one another's greatest cheerleaders and we begin and end each day with love that is both valued and reciprocated. Faith, Family and Focus is the trinity that allows me to establish harmony and fulfillment in my life. As a wife, mother, and career woman, adopting a sense of order and flow among the things that you value is critical. Understanding your values and prioritizing them accordingly allows you to live a life that feels good while honoring and aligning with what matters to you the most; and for me, Faith and Family will always have my Focus.

"Faith & Focus"

Chapter Eight
"Driving Destiny"

In life we are often met with more uncertainty than answers. We may not always know or understand where we are going, but we must trust that we are in fact headed somewhere, and not just anywhere, but somewhere great, worthy and worthwhile. If while peeling back each page, something that I shared resonated with you in any way, consider this the sign that you've been asking and waiting for to take action towards your dreams. Choose to not feel guilty about surviving the hardship that maybe those you love haven't been able to successfully navigate, but instead choose to consider that perhaps you survived so that others can be inspired by your story. Can you imagine that because you had the courage to turn your struggle story into your success story, you activated a will to win, heal or grow within someone who has been able to witness your bravery. I know that success is extremely glamourized in mass media; so much so that people have been convinced that success can be achieved without some sort of suffering. For those of us who took the stairs, we know that it has been the very things that we have suffered through that have conditioned us to manage the weight of success that we benefit from today. Success has been branded as the outcome of desire, but in reality, it's the beauty of what's left after life has tested our will and capacity to handle and manage the things we hope for. Success is the reward for learning from the hard lessons and situations we face and then applying what we've learned in our lives. This is how we truly level up; by taking the bricks that were thrown to break us and using them to build with instead. I should hate the people who molested me and took advantage of my vulnerability. I could easily resent my parents who neglected me; but instead, I choose to extend grace to those who hurt me because God extended that same grace to me but guiding me, protecting me and providing for me along the way. I am so full of gratitude that I've arrived at a place in my life where trauma is so far removed from me, that I have no space for anger or unforgiveness.

Having a pure heart keeps us open to God's abundance and flow of miracles and blessings into our lives; If like me you have made it through things that should have taken you out, then I know that there's a calling on your life and that God has his hands on you, and He has a beautiful plan that is still unfolding. Release the fear, doubt and disappointment that pose as the glue that holds you in your comfort zone, and recognize it for what it is– limitations that are keeping you in bondage to the past; Remember, comfort zones don't keep us safe, they keep us small.

Decide to forge ahead with hope for what is possible, faith for the future and an open heart to receive all the beautiful things that life has for you that trauma can no longer rob you of. Hold on to purpose, it is the thing that we can use to build upon and continue to move forward despite what we have been through. As you decide to take control of your life and step into purpose, you get to redefine family, reevaluate your relationships and create new traditions and opportunities to build new memories. No matter what you have experienced, you are not broken. Instead, you are a masterpiece; a beautiful mosaic of all that you have achieved and survived. You see, because I believe this, I am able to also honor the good attributes that each of my parents instilled in me and how those same values serve me today. For example, my dad set me up for success the best way he knew how. He taught me the value of the dollar and how to save and even manage money. My mother did the best she could and in doing so, she taught me survival and exposed me to the world of dentistry. No matter how bad it seems, the truth is that God can use all of the pieces in your life to design a puzzle of purpose in your life.

Driving Destiny is not just about taking the steering wheel in your life and making the necessary decisions to get you where you want to go, but passing the torch so that others can drive destiny as well. It's about honoring your whole life, even the parts that don't feel good knowing that they too have contributed to who you are today. I wrote this book, not just to share my story, but to remind you that it doesn't matter where you've come from or what you've been through; if you can create a vision for your future and you are willing to work towards it, you can design a life that looks good and feels good. For too long I wore the weight of trauma on my shoulders, then I realized that carrying it all was only weighing me down. I decided that I wanted to do more, be more, achieve more, love more and experience more joy, and I knew that I would have to not only face my trauma, but work through it and heal from it. Doing so has allowed me to build a successful career, create a loving family and make a positive impact in my community.

As you get on board in your own life and begin to steer towards destiny, my hope is that you understand the transformative power of your decisions, relationships, wellness and purpose; and how they all guide in living a meaningful and impactful life. I hope that you are inspired to remain rooted in resilience, so that you may overcome and learn from every challenge, and more than anything, my hope is that you are crowned with purpose. You are here for a reason, there are lives for you to impact, goals for you to achieve and deeper life meaning for you to uncover. Live your life a beautiful act of rebellion, the things that were meant to break you have built you instead. Let faith fortify you and focus ground you. You have survived hard things but now it's time for you to enjoy great things. So go out there and live your best life, make a difference in the world and hold on to your joy.

Resiliently Yours,
~Dr. Christina Monford McNish

Rooted in Resilience
Daily Affirmations

Affirmations are the seeds we plant to nurture a mindset of strength, positivity, and unwavering determination. Just as roots anchor a tree in a storm, affirmations ground us in our beliefs, shaping our perceptions, decisions, and actions. In "Rooted in Resilience," we explore the profound effectiveness of affirmations in fostering resilience and sustaining a perspective aligned with the principles of this book.

Affirmations are not merely wishful thinking; they're a cognitive-behavioral tool backed by science. When we repeat positive statements, our brains respond by forming new neural pathways, rewiring our thinking patterns. Research in neuroscience indicates that affirmations can create a positive bias in our minds, influencing how we perceive ourselves, our capabilities, and the world around us.

Resilience isn't about avoiding adversity but navigating it with strength and adaptability. Affirmations serve as a compass, guiding our thoughts away from self-doubt and negativity, steering them toward confidence, hope, and possibility. By consistently affirming our strengths, values, and goals, we reframe challenges as opportunities for growth rather than insurmountable obstacles.

Self-belief is the cornerstone of resilience. Affirmations bolster our self-esteem and self-worth, reinforcing the belief that we are capable, worthy, and deserving of success and happiness. They act as daily reminders of our inherent potential, instilling a sense of empowerment even in the face of adversity.

In "Rooted in Resilience," we emphasize the importance of aligning actions with values and living a purpose-driven life. Affirmations serve as a bridge between intention and action, reinforcing our commitment to living authentically. By regularly affirming our values and purpose, we strengthen our resolve to make choices that honor them.

ROOTED IN RESILIENCE
DAILY AFFIRMATIONS

1. I am resilient, and I grow stronger with every challenge I face.

2. Success flows to me effortlessly as I work hard and stay committed to my goals.

3. I make decisions with clarity and confidence, guided by my inner wisdom.

4. My relationships are filled with love, trust, and mutual respect.

5. I contribute positively to my community, making an impact daily to help mold the future.

6. I live each moment with purpose, aligning my actions with my values.

7. Challenges are opportunities for growth and learning.

8. I am capable, resourceful, and have everything I need to succeed.

9. I attract abundance in all aspects of my life.

10. I am open to new possibilities and embrace change as a chance for growth.

11. My mindset is optimistic, and I attract positivity into my life.

12. I am deserving of love, happiness, and success.

13. I am surrounded by supportive and encouraging people.

14. I make choices that nourish my mind, body, and soul.

15. I trust myself to overcome obstacles and find solutions.

16. My actions align with my deepest values and beliefs.

17. I radiate confidence and inspire others with my authenticity.

18. I embrace failure as a stepping stone toward success.

19. I am grateful for all the experiences that have shaped me.

20. I am a magnet for positive energy and opportunities.

21. I am capable of creating the life I desire.

22. I choose to focus on what I can control and let go of what I can't.

23. My presence makes a positive impact wherever I go.

24. I am guided by inner strength and wisdom in all that I do.

25. I attract healthy and fulfilling relationships into my life.

26. I am worthy of success, and I attract it effortlessly.

27. I am a source of kindness and compassion in the world.

28. My determination and persistence lead me to success.

29. I embrace challenges as opportunities to learn and grow stronger.

30. I radiate positivity and attract positive experiences.

31. I trust in my ability to make the best decisions for myself.

32. I am constantly evolving and becoming a better version of myself.

33. I am surrounded by love, joy, and abundance.

34. I am enough, just as I am, and I continue to grow and improve.

35. I am a valuable part of my community, making a difference every day.

36. I attract opportunities that align with my purpose and passion.

37. I am open to receiving all the blessings that come my way.

38. My heart is open to giving and receiving love in abundance.

39. I am empowered to create the life I desire.

40. I let go of fear and embrace the unknown with courage.

Rooted in Resilience Mindset Guide

Resilience isn't just about bouncing back; it's about bouncing forward. Adopting A resilient mindset is a way of perceiving and engaging with life's challenges as opportunities for learning, growth, and transformation.

At the core of resilience lies perspective—a lens through which we view adversity. Resilient individuals understand that setbacks and difficulties are part of life's journey, reframing them as temporary hurdles rather than insurmountable barriers. This perspective shift fosters an adaptive mindset, allowing for creative problem-solving and the ability to find silver linings even in the darkest of times.

Resilience isn't an innate trait but a skill that can be cultivated. It involves building inner strength, emotional intelligence, and the capacity to regulate thoughts and emotions. Techniques like mindfulness, self-compassion, and stress management play a pivotal role in nurturing this inner resilience.

A resilient mindset thrives on flexibility and adaptability. It's the ability to bend without breaking, to adjust course when faced with unexpected challenges. Flexibility in thinking allows for the exploration of alternative solutions and the openness to embrace change as an opportunity for growth.

RESILIENCE IMPLEMENTATION GUIDE

Step 1: Self-Reflection and Awareness

- Identify Triggers: Reflect on situations or experiences that challenge your resilience.

- Recognize Thought Patterns: Become aware of negative thought patterns and how they influence your responses to adversity.

Step 2: Mindset Shift

- Reframe Challenges: Practice viewing setbacks as opportunities for learning and growth.

- Positive Self-Talk: Develop a repertoire of positive affirmations to counter negative self-talk.

Step 3: Building Inner Resilience

- Mindfulness Practice:*Dedicate time to mindfulness exercises to strengthen focus and emotional regulation.

- Self-Compassion: Treat yourself with kindness and understanding during difficult times.

Step 4: Flexibility and Adaptability

- Adaptability Exercises: Engage in activities that encourage flexibility, such as trying new experiences or solving problems in unconventional ways.

- Embrace Change: Embrace change as a natural part of life, focusing on the opportunities it presents.

Step 5: Support Network and Resources

- Community Engagement: Foster connections with supportive individuals or groups.

- Educational Resources: Seek books, workshops, or online resources on resilience-building techniques.

Step 6: Practice and Review

- Consistency is Key: Implement these steps consistently and make adjustments based on your experiences.

- Reflection: Periodically assess your progress and make necessary tweaks to your resilience-building strategies.

Rooted in Resilience Mindset Guide

About the Author

Dr. Christina Jade Monford-McNish, born and raised in Jacksonville, Florida. As a cosmetic dentist, Dr. Monford-McNish has been practicing for ten years. Her goal is to provide high quality and compassionate care for the broadest imaginable range of dental care while building meaningful relationships over the course of a lifetime. As a cosmetic dentist, what she enjoys most is being able to transform patient's lives by giving them a new healthy smile, helping them regain confidence in themselves and providing a satisfying dental experience. Dr. Monford-McNish is a member of multiple dental organizations and a member of Delta Sigma Theta Sorority Inc. She is very active in her local community from going to middle and high schools volunteering and speaking to hosting free dental days for those that are in need in the local community to providing $20,000 free smile makeovers. Aside from her day-to-day drilling and filling, Dr. Monford-McNish loves spending time with her family, engaging in impactful community initiatives and inspiring others to adopt resilience as a principle for massive and lasting success. As an inspirational speaker, resilience enthusiast and philanthropist, Dr. Christina works passionately to spread her message in hopes that it will inspire others to overcome opposition, leverage hardships as lessons to grow and make a positive impact in the world. Through her books, speaking engagements and work through her nonprofit organization, she is shifting perspectives centered around adversity, compelling individuals to engage in purpose driven work while honoring the power of resilience and its ability to build tenacity, character and perseverance.

Rooted in Resilience

About the Author